FATAL DOSES

FENTANYL AND OTHER SYNTHETIC OPIOIDS

ANDREA C. NAKAYA

ReferencePoint Press®

San Diego, CA

About the Author

Andrea C. Nakaya, a native of New Zealand, holds a BA in English and an MA in communications from San Diego State University. She has written and edited numerous articles and more than fifty books on current issues. She currently lives in Eagle, Idaho, with her husband and their two children, Natalie and Shane.

Picture Credits:
Cover: Gorodenkoff/Shutterstock.com
 6: Mehmet Dilsiz/Shutterstock.com
10: Steve Heap/Shutterstock.com
13: NurPhoto SRL/Alamy Stock Photo
16: fotoNino/Shutterstock.com
20: Operation 2022/Alamy Stock Photo
23: littlenySTOCK/Shutterstock.com
25: Motortion Films/Shutterstock.com
29: Cum Okolo/Alamy Stock Photo
33: Iryna Inshyna/Shutterstock.com
34: Rawpixel.com/Shutterstock.com
38: Reuters/Alamy Stock Photo
41: Hanson L/Shutterstock.com
44: SeventyFour/Shutterstock.com
48: Damir Khabirov/Shutterstock.com
50: Michael Matthews-Police Images/Alamy
    Stock Photo
54: Rocketclips, Inc./Shutterstock.com

LIBRARY OF CONGRESS CATALOGING-IN-PUBLICATION DATA

Names: Nakaya, Andrea C., 1976- author.
Title: Fatal doses : fentanyl and other synthetic opioids / by Andrea C. Nakaya.
Description: San Diego, CA : ReferencePoint Press, Inc., 2023. | Includes bibliographical references and index.
Identifiers: LCCN 2023009470 (print) | LCCN 2023009471 (ebook) | ISBN 9781678205744 (library binding) | ISBN 9781678205751 (ebook)
Subjects: LCSH: Opioid abuse. | Fentanyl. | Drug abuse.
Classification: LCC RC568.O45 N35 2023 (print) | LCC RC568.O45 (ebook) | DDC 362.29/3--dc23/eng/20230414
LC record available at https://lccn.loc.gov/2023009470
LC ebook record available at https://lccn.loc.gov/2023009471

CONTENTS

When Experimentation Becomes Deadly

Many teenagers say that they have done something risky. Some have tried vaping or alcohol. Others have driven well over the speed limit. It is a popular belief that risky behavior is just a normal part of being a teen. In 2020 Southern California high school student Zach Didier took what he thought was a normal teenage risk; he decided to try a Percocet, a prescription pain reliever that can also cause a euphoric high. Soon after Zach took the pill, his father found him slumped over his desk, not breathing. He could not be revived. Instead of just making him high, Zach's risk killed him. He died because, like thousands of other teens, he did not realize that the drug he experimented with was laced with fentanyl, a synthetic opioid that is far stronger than Percocet. An amount of fentanyl equal in size to only a few grains of salt can be fatal.

In recent years fentanyl and other deadly synthetic opioids have become common in the United States and many other countries. The US Drug Enforcement Administration (DEA) warns that more than 40 percent of illicit prescription pills have fentanyl in them. Taking illegal drugs has always been risky, but now, because fentanyl and other synthetic opioids have become so widespread, teenage experimentation with drugs often turns deadly.

Drug Use Has Become More Risky

Addiction and overdose rates have reached all-time highs in the United States, but an examination of the data reveals that this is not necessarily because more people are taking drugs. For instance, statistics reveal that the number of teens trying illegal drugs has stayed about the same for the past ten years. The National Institute on Drug Abuse's Monitoring the Future survey, a yearly study of drug and alcohol use, shows that in 2021, 32 percent of twelfth graders and almost 19 percent of tenth graders reported that they had used an illicit drug at least once in the past year. Those percentages are similar to what they were in 2011.

However, while drug use has not changed a lot, drug overdose deaths have increased considerably. The Centers for Disease Control and Prevention (CDC) reports that in 2020, about fifty-seven thousand people died as a result of synthetic opioids, a death rate 56 percent higher than the year before. Many of those dying are teens. In a study published in 2022, researchers from the University of California, Los Angeles, used CDC data to show that drug-related deaths nearly doubled in 2020 and increased another 20 percent in the first half of 2021. Reflecting on such statistics, Rahul Gupta, director of the Office of National Drug Control Policy, says, "Each day, we're losing enough people to fill a Boeing 757 passenger jet."[1]

The main cause of this dramatic increase is widely believed to be fentanyl and other synthetic opioids. Addiction expert Joseph Friedman explains that fentanyl has infiltrated the illegal drug market and is making all drug use riskier and potentially deadlier than ever before. While

"Each day, we're losing enough people to fill a Boeing 757 passenger jet."[1]

—Rahul Gupta, director of the Office of National Drug Control Policy the number of teens taking drugs has stayed about the same, more are dying because they are accidentally taking fentanyl. "The increases [in deaths] are almost entirely due to illicit fentanyls, which are increasingly found in counterfeit pills," Friedman says. "These counterfeit pills are spreading across the nation, and teens may not realize they are dangerous."[2] That is exactly how Zach Didier died. "He thought he was experimenting with a pharmaceutical-grade drug," says his mom. "We are losing our kids and all they are doing is experimenting. Fentanyl doesn't even give them a chance."[3] Zach's parents say that they believe his death to be more of a poisoning than an overdose because Zach did not even realize that he was taking fentanyl. "His death was not an addiction death," says Zach's father. "He's a kid who's a victim of fraud."[4]

SYNTHETIC OPIOIDS CAUSE WIDESPREAD HARM

While opioid overdoses are killing thousands of people every year, the flood of synthetic opioids is causing addiction in many more.

A significant number of teens experiment with taking drugs; however, since fentanyl has infiltrated the illegal drug market, this experimentation has become more risky than ever before.

These drugs are highly addictive. According to a 2022 report by the United Nations Office on Drugs and Crime (UNODC), almost half of people who use opioids can develop opioid use disorders, meaning that they cannot stop using opioids even though these drugs are causing them significant harm. The US Department of Health and Human Services estimates that in that same year, 1.6 million Americans were struggling with an opioid use disorder.

> "Fentanyl is the single deadliest drug threat our nation has ever encountered."[5]
>
> —Anne Milgram, administrator of the US Drug Enforcement Administration

Synthetic opioids have been causing so many problems over the past several years that in 2017, the US government declared opioid use to be a public health emergency. DEA administrator Anne Milgram cites the chief culprit: "Fentanyl is the single deadliest drug threat our nation has ever encountered."[5] The United States is not alone. Synthetic opioids are harming hundreds of thousands of people around the world, and the data shows that the problem is only getting worse.

CHAPTER ONE

ALL ABOUT SYNTHETIC OPIOIDS

People have been using natural opioids for thousands of years. The ancient Egyptians, Greeks, and Romans used them to relieve pain, help people sleep, and even soothe crying babies. In 1813 so many people in China were recreationally using opium—the original opioid—and becoming addicted that the government made it illegal to smoke this substance. Germany's Bayer & Co. introduced an opioid called heroin as a pain reliever and cough suppressant in 1898. It was so widely used that Americans could buy it through the popular Sears, Roebuck & Co. mail-order catalog. As medical researchers and the public came to realize that opioids can be dangerous and addictive, lawmakers began to impose many restrictions on their use. However, despite restrictions, opioids continue to be used for a variety of purposes. Opioids are still prescribed in certain painkilling medications, but many opioids—even those used as medical treatments—are abused; others are simply synthesized and sold illegally. The United Nations Office on Drugs and Crime (UNODC) estimates that after cannabis, opioids are the second-most commonly used drug in the world.

WHAT ARE OPIOIDS?

Opioids are chemicals that attach to receptors on nerve cells in the brain and other parts of the body. They make these receptors send signals that tell the brain to block feelings of pain. Opioids are so good at blocking pain that they are prescribed as pain relief for many serious medical conditions, including cancer and chronic pain. Some people also call opioids *narcotics*, a word that comes from a Greek word meaning "to make numb." Unlike some other types of illegal drugs, opioids are "downers," meaning that they do not make people more sociable, energetic, or silly. Instead, they slow people down.

In addition to relieving pain, opioids cause the brain to be flooded with a chemical called dopamine, which causes an intense feeling of pleasure. They can make people feel very happy and relaxed, or "high," and so they are often used recreationally, too. The brain makes its own natural chemicals that control pain and release dopamine, but opioids have a much stronger effect than these natural chemicals. They can create such a pleasurable feeling that people who use them once often want to take them again, and this makes opioids extremely addictive.

If users take too much of an opioid at one time, they can overdose. This is because in addition to reducing feelings of pain and creating a pleasurable high, opioids affect the part of the brain that controls breathing. They can make breathing very slow and shallow, reducing the amount of oxygen that gets to the brain, which in turn can lead to brain damage or even death. Opioids also affect people's awareness and reasoning, so they might not realize that they are having problems breathing.

TYPES OF OPIOIDS

Opioids can be natural or synthetic. Natural opioids come from the opium poppy plant. According to the UNODC, Afghanistan, Myanmar, and Mexico grow more than 95 percent of the world's opium poppies. Morphine, opium, and codeine are all natural opioids. In prescription form they come as a liquid, a pill, or a shot.

Synthetic opioids are manufactured in a laboratory by scientists, who copy the chemical structure of natural opioids. Synthesized variants generally have a more powerful effect than natural ones. Fentanyl is one of the most commonly used synthetic opioids. It is fifty to one hundred times stronger than morphine and is medically used to treat severe pain. Prescription fentanyl comes as a shot, a lozenge or lollipop, or a patch that is applied to the skin. In its prescription form, fentanyl is known by the brand names Actiq, Duragesic, and Sublimaze. There are also numerous fentanyl analogs, which are drugs that have a similar chemical structure to fentanyl. Carfentanil is one. It is one hundred times stronger than fentanyl, and it is used to tranquilize large animals like elephants. Fentanyl is not the only synthetic opioid. There are many others, including tramadol and hydromorphone. Methadone and buprenorphine are synthetic opioids that are used to treat opioid addiction.

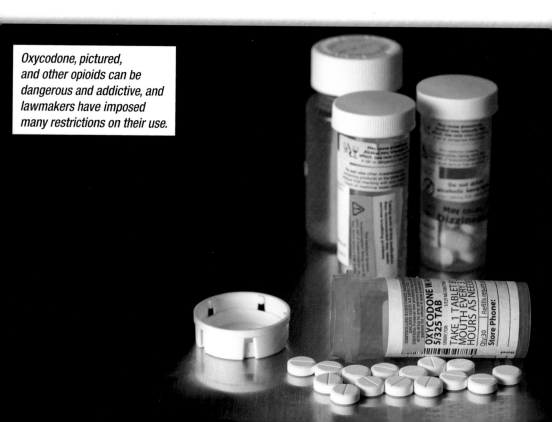

Oxycodone, pictured, and other opioids can be dangerous and addictive, and lawmakers have imposed many restrictions on their use.

Some opioids are classified as semisynthetic, which means that they partially come from natural opioids and are partially made in a laboratory. Semisynthetic opioids include the prescription drugs oxycodone (OxyContin and Percocet) and hydrocodone (Vicodin). Heroin is also a semisynthetic opioid. Unlike most other opioids, heroin no longer has a medically accepted use in the United States or most other parts of the world.

LEGAL AND ILLEGAL USE

Except for heroin, most opioid drugs are used for medical purposes in the United States. Drug companies manufacture them, and they are legally prescribed by doctors, most commonly for severe pain. For example, the American Cancer Society explains, "opioids . . . are often a necessary part of a pain relief plan for cancer patients. These medicines are much like natural substances (called endorphins) made by the body to control pain."[6] A person might also be prescribed an opioid after surgery, to manage chronic pain, or for end-of-life care.

Opioids are also manufactured and sold illegally. Fentanyl is the most common illegal synthetic opioid. Fentanyl and other synthetic opioids are often pressed into counterfeit prescription pills or added to other illicit drugs like heroin or cocaine. Users typically swallow, snort, smoke, or inject synthetic opioids. People take these drugs for many different reasons. Sometimes, synthetic opioid users try to self-medicate for problems such as depression or anxiety. Other people take synthetic opioids because of the pleasurable high these drugs give them. Crystal Long took fentanyl in her twenties because it made her feel good and numbed her worries. "All of your problems go away," she says. "It's like a tingling feeling from head to toe. You're calm. Nothing else matters. There's nothing else around you."[7] No matter what their reason for taking these drugs in the beginning, many people ultimately end up addicted to them, and their new reason for continuing to take them is that they cannot break that addiction.

THE OPIOID CRISIS

In recent years, there has been a huge increase in synthetic opioids—particularly fentanyl—in the drug supply. Large numbers of people use them, are addicted to them, and are dying after overdosing on them. The tragic situation has become a crisis. Most people agree that the opioid crisis started in the late 1990s, when doctors started to write a lot more prescriptions for opioids. This happened for a few different reasons: doctors began to believe that opioids were a more effective way to treat pain; opioids were cheaper and easier than many alternatives, such as physical therapy; and patients started to request them. Critics also charge that drug companies played a major role in increasing prescriptions because they aggressively promoted opioids while greatly understating the risk for addiction.

The Stanford-Lancet Commission is a group of scholars and other experts that was formed to find solutions to the crisis. In a 2022 report, the commission summed up how things got so bad:

Departing from decades of medical practice in which opioids were used mainly for cancer, surgery, and palliative care, US and Canadian regulators, physicians, and dentists expanded opioid prescribing to a broad range of non-cancer pain conditions, from lower back pain to headaches to sprained ankles. Per-person opioid prescribing in morphine milligram equivalents roughly quadrupled between 1999 and 2011. In 2012, medical practitioners in the Canadian and US health-care systems wrote 275 million opioid prescriptions—roughly equivalent to one prescription for each adult in those two nations.[8]

Experts often talk about the opioid crisis having three distinct waves. The first wave was this overprescription of opioids by medical doctors. The second wave began around 2010 and was a result of the first wave. As large numbers of people became addicted to opioids and overdose deaths increased, doctors started to realize that there was a problem and reduced opioid prescriptions. Unfortunately, many people were already addicted to these drugs. Andrew Herring is an emergency physician and director of emergency pain management and addic-

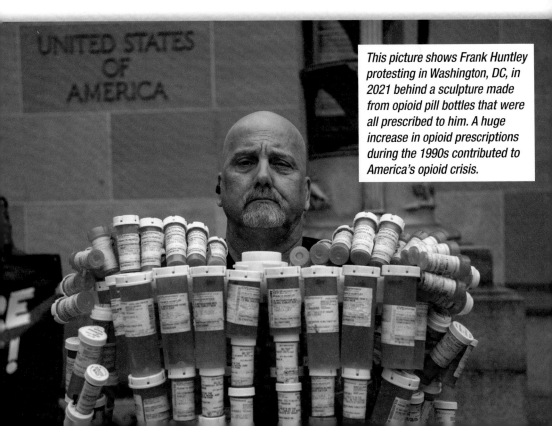

This picture shows Frank Huntley protesting in Washington, DC, in 2021 behind a sculpture made from opioid pill bottles that were all prescribed to him. A huge increase in opioid prescriptions during the 1990s contributed to America's opioid crisis.

tion treatment at Highland Hospital in Oakland, California. He explains that millions of people had become dependent on opioids and that doctors tried to just "turn off" the opioid use without realizing that many of those addicts would simply look elsewhere for drugs. He says, "You cannot just simply say 'no more opioids.' Your body's going to fight you—just like you will fight for air. . . . It was incredibly naïve to think we could, as physicians, as doctors, as health care systems, simply cut people off, without offering treatment." Instead, he says, when doctors reduced the opioid supply, drug dealers stepped in with illegal opioids—particularly heroin—and found many eager customers. Herring states, "There was a demand that no one could have imagined."[9]

FENTANYL INFILTRATES THE DRUG MARKET

The third wave of the crisis started around 2013 as a response to the high demand that doctors were no longer willing to meet. This was when illegal drug makers began to press fentanyl into counterfeit prescription pills and add it to heroin and other drugs they were selling. Fentanyl and other synthetic opioids are cheaper and easier to produce than many other illegal drugs. In addition, because they are so powerful, smaller quantities are needed to produce the same high as other drugs. *New York Times* journalist Sarah Maslin Nir explains how fentanyl gets added to other drugs: "According to interviews with dealers: On each leg of the journey of a drug like heroin or cocaine, from cartel to end user, sellers often cut the pure product with cheap powders that are similar in appearance, a process known as 'stepping on' the drug. Once it was things like baby formula; today, it is likely to be fentanyl." Unfortunately, this process is often inconsistent and haphazard, as she further explains:

14

There is no quality control: A street dealer might cut fentanyl into cocaine that already contains it, creating a lethal dose. In interviews, dealers described lacing as completely ad hoc. One said she measured out fentanyl with a McDonald's ice cream spoon, leveled with a playing card. More than one dealer did not measure at all, spritzing liquid fentanyl onto baking sheets of marijuana.[10]

As a result of the third wave, fentanyl has flooded the drug supply in the United States and many other countries. Researchers conducted interviews in 2021 with people in Oregon who used drugs. Most of the participants said they thought there was a good chance of fentanyl being in the drugs they bought. One interviewee said of fentanyl, "It wasn't here, and now it is. It's everywhere." A heroin user added, "Three years ago, four years ago, I would have never known to ask if fentanyl was in the heroin I was buying. . . . Today, there's more fentanyl-heroin than there is just regular heroin. It's harder to find regular heroin than

WHERE DID FENTANYL COME FROM?

Fentanyl was developed in 1959 by Paul Janssen, a Belgian chemist and founder of Janssen Pharmaceuticals. Janssen had been trying to develop better pain relievers. Journalist Ben Westhoff, author of *Fentanyl, Inc.*, explains: "In 1959, [Janssen] was monkeying around with the chemical structure of morphine and he came upon fentanyl and it had some advantages: It acted faster, it was stronger, and so it quickly became an important medical drug." Starting in 1963, fentanyl was used as an intravenous anesthetic in Europe. After being approved by the US Food and Drug Administration, it was prescribed for the same purpose in the United States. It soon became commonly used for cardio and vascular surgery. In the 1980s a drug company developed a fentanyl skin patch that was used to relieve pain in cancer patients. Soon after that, other fentanyl products were developed, including a lozenge and a tablet. Although medical professionals recognized fentanyl's high risk for abuse among patients, they could not stop the drug from reaching users via mail order from countries like China, Mexico, and India that were quick to increase the illicit supply of a substance that is relatively cheap to produce.

Quoted in Dave Davies, "Fentanyl as a Dark Web Profit Center, from Chinese Labs to U.S. Streets," *Fresh Air*, NPR, September 4, 2019. www.npr.org.

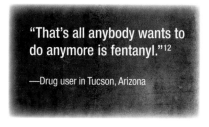
it is to find fentanyl. Fentanyl has flooded the market."[11] Overall, 62 percent of participants reported fentanyl use. In another study, researchers interviewed drug users in Arizona. Almost everyone they talked to said that fentanyl was readily available in the form of pressed pills known as "blues." A woman from Tucson noted, "Blues are everywhere. In the city I live in, they're everywhere. That's all anybody wants to do anymore is fentanyl." A Phoenix man remarked that the reason he started using fentanyl was that it was so easy to get. He said, "I could literally walk out in the apartment courtyard and find three or four people selling blues."[12] As a result of there being so much fentanyl in the drug supply, combined with the fact that it was being added in such a haphazard manner, large numbers of people in the United States started to overdose on this drug. In 2017 the federal government declared the crisis a public health emergency.

That declaration has not stopped the problem. In fact, many experts believe that the United States has entered a fourth wave

A high school student buys drugs. Fentanyl has flooded the drug supply, and when people buy illegal drugs, there is a good chance that they will end up with something contaminated with fentanyl, whether they want it or not.

of the opioid crisis, and they caution that it will be even more deadly. This fourth wave involves the increasing use of stimulants such as cocaine and methamphetamine in combination with fentanyl and other synthetic opioids. It also involves the use of synthetic opioid analogs such as carfentanil. Writer Ross Pomeroy says, "The resulting slurry of intoxicants is so powerful that it's even diminishing the life-saving effects of overdose-reversing drugs like naloxone."[13]

Regardless of how it happened, the fact is that synthetic opioids have become a serious, and growing, problem in the United States and other countries around the world. Like many other worried medical doctors, policy makers, and addiction experts, John McMillan, editor of *American Epidemic: Reporting from the Front Lines of the Opioid Crisis*, warns that this problem cannot be ignored. In the book's introduction he writes, "Know this: However staggering the toll of the epidemic already, it is not yet done. It is probably not even slowing down. The reckoning is far from over."[14]

> "However staggering the toll of the epidemic already, it is not yet done. It is probably not even slowing down."[14]
>
> —John McMillan, book editor

CHAPTER TWO

WHY ARE SYNTHETIC OPIOIDS DANGEROUS?

In 2021 sixteen-year-old Sofia Christoff decided to take half of a Percocet pill that her boyfriend had given her. She had recently tried a few other drugs, including Xanax and Adderall. However, she did not realize that unlike the other pills she had tried, this Percocet was laced with fentanyl. Before she even realized what was happening, she had overdosed. "I'm bored in my room," she says. "I crushed it up, took a line. Felt kind of sparkly for two seconds and then I woke up in the hospital."[15] Luckily for Christoff, her father found her barely breathing, and he called 911. The police officer who arrived was able to administer Narcan, a drug that is used to reverse an opioid overdose. Christoff was then taken to the hospital and later released. Her experience is just one example of how dangerous synthetic opioids are. Christoff says that she feels extremely lucky to still be alive. Unfortunately, many teens are not as lucky as she was. Synthetic opioids cause thousands of people to die of an overdose every year and addiction and health problems in many thousands more. These drugs are so dangerous that they have caused a public health crisis in the United States, where Christoff lives.

UNKNOWN INGREDIENTS

It is very easy to overdose on synthetic opioids because they are so concentrated. Only a tiny dose can be fatal. *Science* writer Kathleen McLaughlin says, "For most individuals, a lethal fentanyl dose is about 2 milligrams—an amount so minuscule that in a test tube it looks like a few grains of salt clinging to the glass."[16] She adds that carfentanil, a fentanyl analog that is sometimes found in illegal drugs, is one hundred times stronger. A fentanyl overdose can also happen very quickly, within minutes or even seconds. This means that there is often only a very short window of time to take action to treat the overdose and stop a person from dying. People who do not regularly take opioids are particularly sensitive to these drugs and can overdose more easily than people who take them on a regular basis.

Unless it is a prescription product that comes directly from a pharmacy, it is very difficult to know whether a drug contains a deadly amount of fentanyl or other synthetic opioid. Most synthetic opioids do not have a specific taste or smell, and drugs with opioids look the same as drugs without them. Furthermore, the DEA explains that the amount of fentanyl in illicit drugs can vary widely, which makes it even more difficult for users to know what they are getting. The DEA explains, "Producing illicit fentanyl is not an exact science. . . . DEA analysis has found counterfeit pills ranging from .02 to 5.1 milligrams (more than twice the lethal dose) of fentanyl per tablet." The agency stresses that even pills that look like they are prescription pills can be fake, stating, "Unless a drug is prescribed by a licensed medical professional and dispensed by a legitimate pharmacy, you can't know if it's fake or legitimate. And without laboratory testing, there's no way to know the amount of fentanyl in an individual pill or how much may have been added to another drug."[17]

> "Unless a drug is prescribed by a licensed medical professional and dispensed by a legitimate pharmacy, you can't know if it's fake or legitimate."[17]
>
> —US Drug Enforcement Administration

19

Overdose Deaths

Every year, hundreds of thousands of Americans use synthetic opioids, a rate far higher than any other nation in the world. Journalist Andrew Sullivan writes, "No other developed country is as devoted to the poppy as America. We consume 99 percent of the world's hydrocodone and 81 percent of its oxycodone. We use an estimated 30 times more opioids than is medically necessary for a population our size."[18]

The CDC collects overdose statistics in the United States, and it finds that overdoses from synthetic opioids—already significant—are becoming even more common. According to the agency, from 1999 to 2020, synthetic opioid overdoses increased substantially in the United States, with the rate of increase at 56 percent. It reports that in 2020, 57,834 people died from overdoses involving synthetic opioids. According to provisional CDC data, in 2021 that number reached 71,238. The agency reports that synthetic opioids are the drugs that are most common in overdose deaths. For instance, in 2020 almost three-quarters of drug overdose deaths involved an opioid.

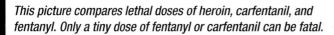

This picture compares lethal doses of heroin, carfentanil, and fentanyl. Only a tiny dose of fentanyl or carfentanil can be fatal.

HEROIN　　　**CARFENTANIL**　　　**FENTANYL**

TRANQ CONTAMINATION CAUSES EVEN MORE HEALTH PROBLEMS

In some parts of the United States, drug users are finding that the fentanyl they buy is contaminated with an animal tranquilizer called xylazine, which many drug users refer to as "tranq." Tranq causes sores at the injection sites that build up painful mounds of dead tissue. Many drug users let these aching sores get worse and worse because they are too embarrassed to seek treatment. However, if treatment of the wounds is left too long, physicians might have no recourse but to amputate the infected limbs. Most users are afraid of tranq-laced drugs, but they face the risk because they crave fentanyl. Brooke Peder is a thirty-eight-year-old tattoo artist and addict. Her right leg was amputated because of an infection from a tranq wound. Unfortunately, she continues to use the drug, injecting into her arm several times a day—even though that now has a large sore—because she is afraid to cause a new wound anywhere else on her body. Journalist Jan Hoffman says, "She unrolled a bandage from elbow to palm. Beneath patches of blackened tissue, exposed white tendons and pus, the seared flesh was hot and red."

Jan Hoffman, "Tranq Dope: Animal Sedative Mixed with Fentanyl Brings Fresh Horror to U.S. Drug Zones," *New York Times*, January 7, 2013. www.nytimes.com.

LASTING HEALTH PROBLEMS

Even if a person does not die from an opioid overdose, it can still cause serious health problems. Many drug users experience non-fatal overdoses—a type of overdose that is more common than a fatal overdose—and these can cause long-lasting problems. When people overdose on opioids, their breathing can slow down or stop, meaning that insufficient oxygen gets to the brain. This can cause permanent brain damage. Amanda Wright survived a fentanyl overdose in 2017; however, she was left with permanent brain damage. Journalists Jodie Martinson and Bridgette Watson share her story. After the overdose, they say, "Amanda was alive, but she was not the same. She couldn't remember how to brush her teeth or take a shower, and she stared blankly at her mom when asked basic questions. 'Are you having trouble coming up with an answer?' Liana Wright would ask after prolonged pauses. All her daughter could do was nod her head back at her."[19] Two years, later, Amanda learned to hold a conversation with her mother again; however, Martinson and Watson note that she will probably never be able to live alone or hold a job, and her mother stresses that she is not the same person as she was before the overdose. According to her mother, "She's Amanda with the dimmer switch turned down a bit."[20]

There is also evidence that nonfatal overdoses can result in a gradual deterioration of brain cells. In a paper published in the *International Journal of Drug Policy* in 2021, researchers explain that they found evidence that nonfatal overdoses can lead to a deterioration of brain cells that resembles the onset of Alzheimer's disease. Janna Ataiants, one of the authors of the study, says, "Many people still think of opioid overdose as a strictly life-or-death issue, but fatal overdoses constitute only 3–4% of all overdoses and repeated nonfatal overdoses may have far-reaching consequences for survivors. We need to acknowledge how nonfatal overdoses attack brain cells, perhaps to the point of bringing on symptoms similar to those of Alzheimer's disease."[21]

EXTREMELY ADDICTIVE

Synthetic opioids are also dangerous because they are very addictive. When users take an opioid regularly, over time they build up tolerance, so that a greater and greater amount of the drug is needed in order to produce the same results. The National Institute on Drug Abuse explains, "Drug dependence occurs with repeated use, causing the neurons to adapt so they only function normally in the presence of the drug."[22] Most opioid users become addicted. This addiction is known as opioid use disorder. The American Psychiatric Association provides a practical yet unsettling definition:

> [Opioid use disorder is] a problematic pattern of opioid use leading to problems or distress, with at least two of the following occurring within a 12-month period:
>
> 1. Taking larger amounts or taking drugs over a longer period than intended.

2. Persistent desire or unsuccessful efforts to cut down or control opioid use.
3. Spending a great deal of time obtaining or using the opioid or recovering from its effects.
4. Craving, or a strong desire or urge to use opioids.
5. Problems fulfilling obligations at work, school or home.
6. Continued opioid use despite having recurring social or interpersonal problems.
7. Giving up or reducing activities because of opioid use.
8. Using opioids in physically hazardous situations.
9. Continued opioid use despite ongoing physical or psychological problems likely to have been caused or worsened by opioids.
10. Tolerance (i.e., need for increased amounts or diminished effect with continued use of the same amount).
11. Experiencing withdrawal (opioid withdrawal syndrome) or taking opioids (or a closely related substance) to relieve or avoid withdrawal symptoms.[23]

Teens with opioid use disorder often struggle in school due to depression, lack of sleep, or poor class attendance.

The American Psychiatric Association explains that opioid use disorder differs from some other types of substance use disorders in that people can become physically dependent in a very short period—as little as a month or two—and can experience severe physical symptoms when they try to stop. The organization says, "[Withdrawal symptoms include] generalized pain, chills, cramps, diarrhea, dilated pupils, restlessness, anxiety, nausea, vomiting, insomnia, and very intense cravings. Because these symptoms are severe it creates significant motivation to continue using opioids to prevent withdrawal."[24] According to a 2022 report by the UNODC, 46.6 percent of people who use opioids develop opioid use disorders. The report says that many do so within two years of starting to use.

Opioids can be so addictive that even when people are suffering very negative consequences, they continue to use these drugs. A user named Jessica says of addiction, "It isn't a choice, and it isn't fun. By the time you are fully addicted, you are a slave to the chemicals. Addiction doesn't care about your kids. It doesn't care

LOOKING FOR FENTANYL

When fentanyl was first discovered in illicit drugs, many users tried to avoid it because it is such a powerful and risky drug. That has changed. In recent years, there are widespread reports that more and more drug users prefer fentanyl and actively look for it. Kristen Marshall, who runs a drug testing program for the National Harm Reduction Coalition, explains the logic behind this change: "Fentanyl is stronger, you need less of it, and it's cheaper. So why wouldn't I, as somebody with limited funds, want to spend my money on something that's a better value and therefore a better product?" The economics of fentanyl use seem to outweigh its addictive properties and the risk that the drug is laced with other dangerous substances. Many addicts also report that after using fentanyl, it can be hard to go back to using other drugs because they do not get the same high. Therefore, they continue to assume the risks of overdosing or incurring other serious medical problems.

Quoted in Christine Vestal, "Some Drug Users in Western U.S. Seek Out Deadly Fentanyl. Here's Why," Pew Charitable Trusts, January 7, 2019. www.pewtrusts.org.

about your relationships. The only thing addiction knows is that it is hungry and you WILL feed it."[25] Journalist Eric Rankin interviewed twenty-two-year-old fentanyl addict Kati Mather. She told him that she has overdosed eleven times, but she is still unable to stop using fentanyl. Her face is covered in self-inflicted wounds from the times when she has been unable to get fentanyl and feeling withdrawal symptoms. Rankin says, "When I first see her face, I think she's been badly beaten. Her forehead and chin are covered in blood."[26] However, he quickly discovers that she made the wounds by scratching her own face.

An All-Consuming Obsession

BoardPrep Recovery, an addiction and mental health treatment center, explains how fentanyl becomes all-consuming. BoardPrep's representatives say, "Do you know what it is like to be distracted by something so much that it was hard for you to stop looking at it? Pre-occupied with hunger and unable to focus on anything but your growling stomach? Stuck in your thoughts about a relationship? Ever just want to 'change the channel' but you couldn't? Yes? Multiply that feeling by 10 or 100. Fentanyl addiction is like that."[27]

Researchers interviewed people who lived in Arizona and had used illegal opioids. These users' stories echoed the idea that fentanyl quickly becomes the only thing that an addict thinks about. One man said, "When you do smoke a fentanyl pill and you're good for a little while, and then you gotta smoke another one. You're good for a little while, and then the times get shorter and shorter." A woman reiterated, "It's very addictive. . . . I've had a lot of people tell me that it's almost impossible to get off of. That's what I heard."[28]

BoardPrep Recovery explains that fentanyl becomes so important to addicts that they will do anything to keep using it. The center says, "The addicted brain responds to the idea of cutting back or quitting the drug as a threat to survival. The using brain quickly dismisses the idea, rationalizing and justifying reasons for continued use. The brain crafts excuses, making continued drug use seem like the right thing to do."[29] Twenty-year-old Isaac agrees that addicts will do anything to keep using. He says that he started using fentanyl when he was eighteen years old, and at the height of his addiction, he was taking five or six pills a day. "I remember doing crimes just to get it," he says. "When I was in my Fentanyl addiction, you name it, I would do it. There's not much I wouldn't do for Fentanyl, honestly."[30]

> "The current opioid crisis ranks as one of the most devastating public health catastrophes of our time."[31]
>
> —Howard K. Koh, Harvard Kennedy School professor

A PUBLIC HEALTH CRISIS

Synthetic opioids are so dangerous that they have caused a public health crisis in the United States that is harming hundreds of thousands of people. In its 2022 report, the Stanford-Lancet Commission stated that in the United States and Canada, the opioid-related mortality rate since 1999 is higher than the worst year of the HIV/AIDS epidemic. One of its members, Howard K. Koh, is a Harvard Kennedy School professor. He says, "The current opioid crisis ranks as one of the most devastating public health catastrophes of our time."[31]

CHAPTER THREE

How Synthetic Opioids Are Altering Society

According to data from the CDC, life expectancy in the United States decreased by almost a year from 2020 to 2021. The year before, it declined by almost two years. Grant Baldwin, director of the division of overdose prevention at the CDC's National Center for Injury Prevention and Control, claims that such a decline is extraordinary. According to Baldwin, "This is the first time this [has] happened in over a hundred years. The last time was when we last experienced the pandemic: the 1918 flu pandemic." While this decrease has a number of causes, including the COVID-19 pandemic, synthetic opioids are widely believed to be a major culprit. Baldwin says, "The epidemic, the impact of the opioid epidemic is so pronounced . . . [and it is] something I expect to continue."[32] The decrease in US life expectancy is just one way that synthetic opioids are altering society. Overall, these drugs are harming both individuals and society in many ways.

Negative Health Effects

On an individual level, the long-term use of synthetic opioids can have a wide range of negative health impacts. These drugs can cause gastrointestinal problems such as abdominal cramping, bloating, or chronic constipation. They can also negatively affect the respiratory system, causing slowed or irregular breathing. Some studies show that opioid users are more likely to experience anxiety, depression, or other mental health problems. There is also research linking opioids to liver damage, an increased risk of fractures, circulatory system problems, and harm to the reproductive system. In addition, people who inject opioids are susceptible to several different infectious diseases, including the human immunodeficiency virus (HIV), that are spread by using needles. For example, in its 2022 report, the UNODC said that people who inject opioids also have a significant risk of becoming infected with hepatitis C, an infectious disease that can cause serious liver damage.

Overall, the UNODC report shows that out of all the many types of drugs people take, opioids are responsible for 77 percent of drug deaths worldwide. The agency found that people who use opioids for nonmedical purposes have a much higher risk of dying prematurely. UNODC researchers tracked opioid users and found that a quarter to half of those whom the agency tracked were deceased within twenty years. The report main-tains that "[the] mortality rate is about 10–20 times higher in opioid users than among the general population of the corresponding age and sex."[33]

ADDICTION IN BABIES BORN TO OPIOID USERS

Synthetic opioids can also harm people who are not even using them. For instance, when a mother continues to use opioids throughout her pregnancy, it can harm her fetus in many ways. Babies born to opioid users are more likely to have numerous health problems and can even be born addicted to opioids themselves. *Neonatal opioid withdrawal syndrome (NOWS)* is the medical term for when a baby is born with opioid withdrawal symptoms. Some people also use the term *neonatal abstinence syndrome (NAS)*, which can be caused by prenatal exposure to a variety of other drugs in addition to opioids. Babies who have NOWS or NAS can be irritable and have seizures, respiratory problems, and trouble feeding. According to HealthyChildren, a website of the

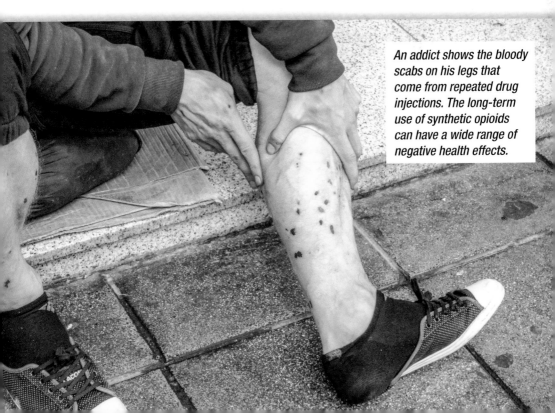

An addict shows the bloody scabs on his legs that come from repeated drug injections. The long-term use of synthetic opioids can have a wide range of negative health effects.

American Academy of Pediatrics, "Facing lengthy hospital stays, babies with NOWS are more likely to have low birthweight, trouble breathing and eating, seizures and tremors, and can experience long-term problems with learning and behavior."[34] The academy says that NOWS is very common, and a baby with NOWS or NAS is born every fifteen minutes in the United States. In a study published in 2021 in the *Journal of the American Medical Association*, researchers reported on the rate of pregnant women who had opioid use disorder and babies who were born with opioid withdrawal symptoms. The researchers found that from 2010 to 2017, cases of babies born with opioid withdrawal symptoms increased by 82 percent and cases of pregnant women with an opioid use disorder rose by 131 percent.

Samantha Powell was addicted to opioids when she gave birth to her daughter Luna. In an ABC News interview, she explains that child protective services took Luna away and would not let Powell see her for a month. She recalls, "It was devastating; I love my daughter. The guilt and the shame it's something that you cannot describe."[35] According to Powell, she felt so terrible that she even started to think that maybe her daughter would be better off without her.

Economic Costs

Opioid abuse and addiction also have substantial economic costs. In a 2022 report, the Congressional Budget Office discusses these costs and concludes that they are so large that they have significantly affected the federal budget. It explains that opioid abuse lowers participation in the labor force, which reduces people's earning and spending power and decreases corporate productivity. Opioid abuse also means that the government is forced to spend more on treating opioid-related health problems, addiction, and overdoses. It also needs to spend money on preventing the illegal trafficking of these drugs and on child welfare and other social programs that help people affected by abuse and addiction.

Opioid Abuse in Kentucky

While opioid abuse is a major problem throughout the United States, some states have been hit harder than others. Kentucky is one of the states bearing the brunt of the crisis. The National Institutes of Health HEAL Initiative claims, "Kentucky is ground zero of the opioid overdose epidemic." It reports that Kentucky has one of the highest rates of opioid overdose deaths in the country, and that nine in ten Kentuckians who are struggling with a substance use disorder do not receive treatment. Nikki King, who grew up in southeastern Kentucky, says that opioid abuse was very common in her community. According to King:

> The first time I saw an overdose, I already knew what to do, because we had talked about it so much at school with my friends, and I was 13. At the time, I was proud of myself for knowing what to do and for listening to those conversations. And I look back and I thought, why did a 13-year-old know how to wake somebody up from an opioid overdose? Like that should not ever happen, yet that was just part of our normal day-to-day conversation.

National Institutes of Health HEAL Initiative, "Kentucky: State Snapshot." https://healing communitiesstudy.org.

Quoted in Hari Sreenivasan, "How Nikki King Is Innovating Treatment for Opioid Addiction," PBS, February 8, 2021. www.pbs.org.

Estimates of the exact costs vary, but they are in the billions of dollars. For instance, according to a 2021 report by the CDC, in 2017 the opioid epidemic cost the United States $1 trillion, which includes $471 billion for treating opioid use disorder and $550 billion for opioid overdoses. The Pew Charitable Trusts' Substance Use Prevention and Treatment Initiative estimates that in 2021 there were $14.8 billion in criminal justice costs related to opioids and $92 billion in lost productivity.

Destruction of Families and Friendships

Synthetic opioids can also destroy personal relationships. When people become addicted to opioids, these drugs become the most important thing in their lives, and addicts will ignore everything else around them such as school, jobs, friends, and family. A former addict named Wendy explains how her addiction made her forget about everything else that had mattered to her:

I was a Registered Nurse. I never imagined that I could become addicted to opiates . . . lose everything I owned. I wound up homeless, on public assistance. Lost my license to practice, was chronically in trouble, in court, arrested. My life went from comfortably upper-middle class to indigent in less than six months. I used to be judgmental. I used to say, "I would never do that!" I would have the public know. . . . Don't judge. Never see yourself as someone who "would never."[36]

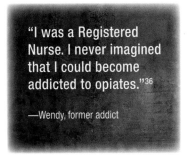

"I was a Registered Nurse. I never imagined that I could become addicted to opiates."[36]

—Wendy, former addict

The sister of an addict echoes this theme of obsession with opioids to the exclusion of everything else. She relates, "My little sister was in college, on the golf team and getting straight As. Now she has been to prison, convicted of felonies, lost everything in her life including her relationships with us, her family and is living on the streets."[37]

When parents use opioids, it can devastate their family, with parents often so focused on their drug use that they fail to properly care for their children. In some cases parents are so neglectful that their children end up in the welfare system. Marian Wright Edelman, founder and president emerita of the Children's Defense Fund, explains some of the many ways that children are harmed by parents who use opioids:

From the earliest days of pregnancy children whose parents abuse opioids are at high risk. In addition to prenatal drug exposure, parents distracted by drugs and without help may be unable to provide children necessary care to grow and thrive. Children and teens are also susceptible to accidental opioid exposure and misuse. Whether children are born suffering from drug exposure, their parents' addiction struggle leads to toxic stress or involvement with the child welfare system, or they use or are accidentally exposed to drugs themselves, opioid addiction has a devastating impact.[38]

Further, when parents use opioids, their children can be more likely to do so themselves when they get older.

Paris Hardee's father was addicted to opioids when she was a child, and her life was negatively impacted by that addiction. She says that he was arrested in front of her and her friends when she was about eight years old. "We lost all of our friends," she says. "Nobody's parents would let us play with them after that and we had to move. That's really hard when you're in the third grade. I lost every friend I had." Hardee says that no matter how much she tried to love and support him, she realized that when her father was using opioids, he would always put the drugs before

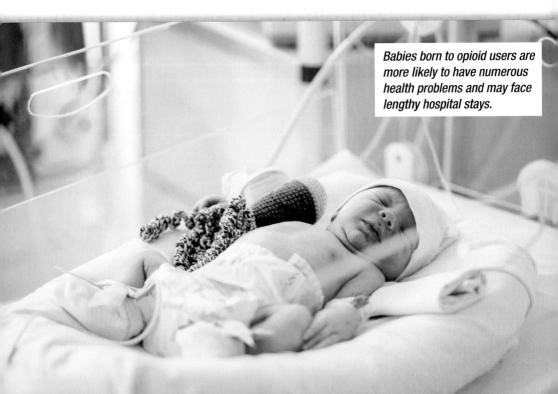

Babies born to opioid users are more likely to have numerous health problems and may face lengthy hospital stays.

his family. "He was always going to choose drugs over health, over family, over friendships," she says, "He was going to choose drugs no matter what."[39]

AT-RISK GROUPS

Synthetic opioids are extremely harmful to all sectors of American society; however, statistics show that certain groups of people are feeling the effects disproportionately. The Stanford-Lancet Commission's 2022 report identifies the groups most affected by this crisis. It states that in the United States and Canada, males and young-to-middle-aged people have the highest rates of opioid use. The commission also reports, "People experiencing homelessness and those recently released from incarceration have been hit particularly hard throughout the crisis, and the frequency of overdose mortality is shockingly high in these populations."[40] Other studies have shown that veterans are more likely to overdose on opioids. Experts believe this is related to the fact that many use opioids to manage the chronic pain or trauma that they have from war injuries or combat experiences.

A homeless woman sleeps on the sidewalk. The rate of fatal opioid overdoses is high among the homeless population in the United States.

In the early years of the opioid crisis, White non-Hispanics had the highest rate of opioid-related problems; however, research shows that synthetic opioids now have a substantial effect on minorities, too. The Stanford-Lancet Commission notes that the rate of fatal overdoses among African Americans has increased significantly in recent years and that it "is now on par with that among white, and American Indian and Alaska Native populations."[41] In a 2022 article in *Drug Science, Policy and Law*, researchers analyzed opioid-related deaths. They also found that US minority groups are experiencing extremely high rates of opioid-related deaths. The researchers state that while the opioid crisis is still frequently depicted in the media as something affecting White, non-Hispanic communities, there has been a historic surge in overdose deaths among US minorities in urban communities. The researchers examined CDC data from 1999 to 2017 and report that opioid-related deaths among Hispanics increased from 3.5 per 1,000 people to 6.8 per 1,000 people during that period. For Blacks, the increase was from 3.5 to 12.9 per 1,000 people. The researchers argue that not recognizing these increases is extremely harmful to Black and Hispanic communities because it means the people in these communities are not as likely to be included in prevention outreach and treatment efforts.

> "If we don't stop the fentanyl and opioid abuse, it is going to destroy generations to come."[42]
>
> —Eric Adams, mayor of New York City

WIDESPREAD DEVASTATION

Overall, synthetic opioids are causing widespread devastation throughout the entire United States. They are harming people of all ages, including children and other family members who are not using the drugs themselves. Synthetic opioids are also costing the nation billions of dollars. "If we don't stop the fentanyl and opioid abuse, it is going to destroy generations to come," says New York City mayor Eric Adams, "Fentanyl is destroying our cities across America. We have to fight back and stop it."[42]

CHAPTER FOUR

TREATING AND PREVENTING OVERDOSE AND ADDICTION

Michael Morton was in eleventh grade when he tried fentanyl for the first time. He ate some of the gel from a prescription fentanyl patch that he had stolen from the pharmacy where he worked. "I fell back in my seat and I fell in love," he says, "It was the best high I ever had." Morton loved the high so much that he continued to use fentanyl even though he often passed out from it and came close to overdosing many times. It was not until four fellow drug users died that he finally decided to quit. He says that six years later, staying clean is still a struggle. "The urge always comes back,"[43] he main-tains. Fentanyl and other synthetic opioids are power-ful drugs that are easy to become addicted to and to overdose on. However, there are ways both to prevent an opioid overdose and to treat one after it has oc-curred. There are also numerous options for avoiding and treating opioid addiction.

Overdosing on Opioids

Opioids affect the part of a person's brain that regulates breathing. Overdoses happen when users take too much of an opioid and it slows down or stops their breathing. This can lead to unconsciousness or death. Besides reduced breathing, some of the common symptoms of an overdose are trouble staying awake or talking, gray or blue lips or nails, a slow heartbeat, cold and clammy skin, small pupils, and unconsciousness. Tyrone Riley works at a shelter in Trenton, New Jersey. He once found his cousin, Lamar, slumped and unconscious on the floor from an overdose. "I shook him," says Riley, "But he didn't respond. He was in a weird state. His eyes were looking up in his head. And he had turned blue."[44] Another user known as Owen (not his real name) also witnessed an opioid overdose. He recalls:

> My friends used and maybe [a] half hour or so later one of my friends was making a funny noise, like he had something in his throat. I went to check on him and I couldn't get him to answer me. Normally when someone's used you can get a response, maybe not speaking, but they will look at you. Anyway I watched him for a while and his breathing seemed to be getting quieter again, really weak. I called his name and shook him but he didn't wake up.[45]

An opioid overdose can happen for many different reasons. A person can overdose by taking a drug that was prescribed for someone else or taking a drug without knowing how strong it is, such as one purchased illegally from a drug dealer. An overdose can also result from mixing opioids with other drugs or alcohol or from taking an opioid medication in a way that it is not intended to be used, such as snorting a crushed extended-release pill rather than swallowing it whole. No matter what the reason, though, an overdose is an emergency that can quickly lead to death if nothing is done. Daniel Colby, an assistant professor and co-medical

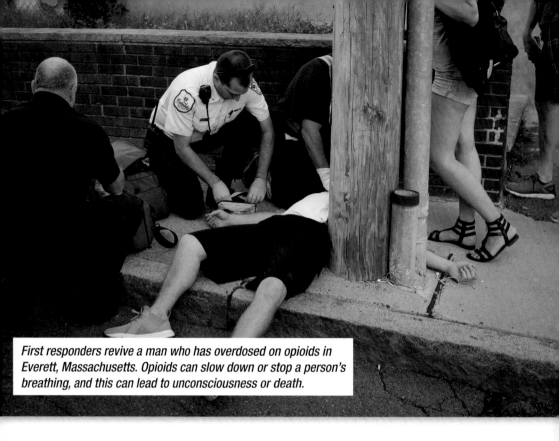

First responders revive a man who has overdosed on opioids in Everett, Massachusetts. Opioids can slow down or stop a person's breathing, and this can lead to unconsciousness or death.

director for the Department of Emergency Medicine at UC Davis Health, says, "If you find someone who has overdosed on fentanyl or another opioid, you should call 911 immediately."[46]

TREATING AN OVERDOSE

An opioid overdose can be reversed with a medicine called naloxone, which is sold under the brand name Narcan. Naloxone attaches to opioid receptors in the body and blocks the effects of opioids. If a person's breathing has slowed or stopped because of an opioid overdose, Naloxone can bring it back to normal. This drug is administered as either an injection or a nasal spray. An overdose may be so severe that a rescuer might have to administer multiple doses of naloxone. In some states, naloxone has only been available with a prescription, which

"If you find someone who has overdosed on fentanyl or another opioid, you should call 911 immediately."[46]

—Daniel Colby, co-medical director for the Department of Emergency Medicine at UC Davis Health

38

has limited access to this drug. However in March 2023, the US Food and Drug Administration approved Narcan nasal spray for over-the-counter, nonprescription use. This will make it easier for many people to access it.

One woman tells the story of using naloxone to reverse an overdose in her twenty-year-old daughter, Callie. She says that after finding her daughter unresponsive in bed, she administered a dose into Callie's thigh. She says, "There was nothing, no sign of life. Her teeth were clenched and my husband couldn't get [his] breaths into her mouth. My son was performing such hard chest compressions I thought her bones would break. . . . We were lucky the kit came with two doses. I shot her again in the thigh. Suddenly her tightly clenched jaw released and my husband was able to get some air into her."[47] She says that a first responder arrived soon after that and administered even more

CAN YOU OVERDOSE BY TOUCHING FENTANYL?

In recent years there have been stories circulating about becoming high or overdosing on fentanyl just by touching it or breathing it in. Scott Phillips is a medical toxicologist and medical director of the Washington Poison Center. He says that despite all the stories, this is highly unlikely. According to Phillips, cases in which people believe this has happened are more likely to be a reaction of fear. He explains:

> People are afraid of this stuff. It doesn't matter if you're a scientist, chemist, police officer or bystander, fear can be a reaction in response to situations. We've seen that often the symptoms people report aren't characteristic of fentanyl intoxication. It might be a headache or lightheadedness. There is a known reaction called 'nocebo,' when there isn't a biological or physical reason for a response, but a person experiences symptoms. It could be a reaction to a stressful situation, but it's doubtful that it would be fentanyl intoxication.

> Phillips stresses that if somebody witnesses an overdose, he or she should not be afraid to help, because they are unlikely to be harmed by being in close contact with a fentanyl overdose victim.

Quoted in Public Health Insider, "It's Safe to Give Help: Questions and Answers About Secondhand Fentanyl Exposure," April 5, 2022. https://publichealthinsider.com.

doses of naloxone until her daughter finally started to breathe and move. She even started to cry and tried to talk. Callie's mom says the first responders told her that the doses of naloxone that she administered saved her daughter's life.

NALOXONE DISTRIBUTION

In the United States there is controversy over whether naloxone should be more widely available to the general public, especially for people who are likely to overdose or to witness an overdose. Many people insist that quite simply, distributing naloxone decreases opioid-related deaths, and so it should be more widely distributed. The National Institute on Drug Abuse explains:

> Naloxone is a safe medication that is widely used by emergency medical personnel and other first responders to prevent opioid overdose deaths. Unfortunately, by the time a person having an overdose is reached, it is often too late. . . . Naloxone distribution programs give naloxone kits to opioid users, their friends and families, and others who may find themselves in a position to save the life of someone at risk of an opioid overdose.[48]

Critics contend that making kits more widely available is not a good solution because it does nothing to reduce use, and so overdoses will keep happening. In one 2020 study, researchers interviewed a number of people who had obtained free naloxone kits and later used them to help peers. While the researchers found evidence that these kits save lives, they also found evidence that increasing the availability of kits does not change people's behavior. For instance, some of those interviewed said that while they might temporarily reduce their use after being revived from an overdose, their long-term behavior

"Naloxone is a safe medication that is widely used by emergency medical personnel and other first responders to prevent opioid overdose deaths."[48]

—National Institute on Drug Abuse

40

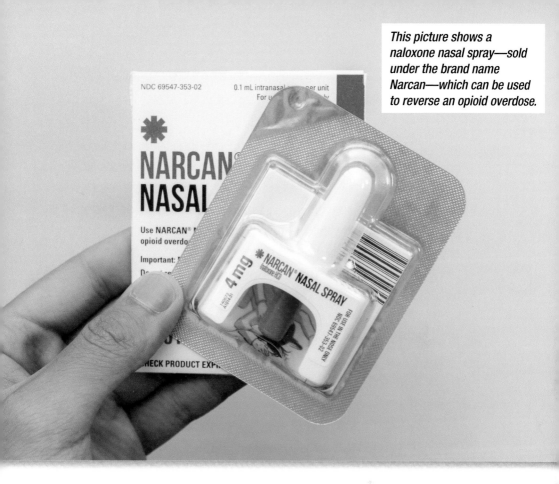

This picture shows a naloxone nasal spray—sold under the brand name Narcan—which can be used to reverse an opioid overdose.

did not change. The researchers add, "A few participants thought people were less cautious about their drug use because of the availability of naloxone. According to one person, 'People feel like they don't have to be as careful when using when having [naloxone] around.'"[49]

FENTANYL TEST STRIPS

While naloxone is used to treat an overdose after it has occurred, there are also ways to prevent one from occurring in the first place. A chief reason that an increasing number of people are overdosing on opioids is that illicit fentanyl has infiltrated the drug supply. As a result, users often do not realize that their drugs contain fentanyl, and they overdose by accident. Fentanyl test strips help with this problem because they allow users to test drugs for fentanyl before using. Giselle Appel, Brenna Farmer, and Jonathan Avery from Weill Cornell Medicine explain how fentanyl test strips work:

> They are inexpensive ($1 each), simple to use, and can be carried in a wallet or purse. The single-use strips work like other over-the-counter testing products: The user dips the strip into water containing a small amount of well-mixed drug residue and waits a few minutes for the result. The appearance of a single line signifies the presence of fentanyl or fentanyl analogues such as acetylfentanyl, and two red lines signifies its absence.[50]

While test strips are widely available in some states, in many they are illegal because they are considered to be drug paraphernalia.

Even in places where they are legal, fentanyl test strips are controversial. Proponents insist that they reduce fentanyl overdoses. While the tests do not reveal exactly how much fentanyl is in a drug, they do allow users to make a better-educated choice about what to do next. If the drug tests positive for fentanyl, they can use less of it, use a different batch, or make sure that they use it in the presence of other people and have naloxone available. Research shows that many people do make safer choices after using test strips. For instance, in a study published in 2018, researchers recruited ninety-three young adult drug users in Rhode Island and gave them rapid fentanyl test strips to use. They later asked the users about their experiences with the test strips and whether testing affected their behavior. While few of the participants reported getting rid of their drugs after receiving a positive result, a significant percentage said that they used smaller amounts, went slower, or used with someone else.

While there is evidence that fentanyl test strips can make users more cautious, many people are still opposed to the distribution of these strips. One of the biggest complaints is that fentanyl tests might send the message that it is okay to use a drug if it tests free of fentanyl. Another problem is that some addicts use the kits to find drugs that contain fentanyl. Takeya Brittingham works for Bmore POWER, a nonprofit organization connected to the Baltimore City Health Department. She explains that many addicts want drugs that have fentanyl in them. "That's what they chase," she says. "They want it because somebody overdosed on it. That means it's good [i.e., potent]."[51] Finally, critics point out that the kits are not completely reliable. The test strips can show incorrect results if users test improperly or read the results incorrectly, and the results can be affected by the presence of methamphetamine in a drug and so be misread.

Medications for Opioid Addiction

While test strips and naloxone can help reduce the harms of opioid overdose, many people agree that the best way to address the problem is to treat the addiction that causes people to overdose in the first place. Most opioid addicts trying to get sober take medication to help them do so. There are three different prescription medications approved by the US Food and Drug Administration for treating addiction to opioids: methadone, buprenorphine, and naltrexone. Methadone and buprenorphine attach to the same opioid receptors in the brain that opioid drugs do, and

Teens participate in a therapy session. Addicts trying to beat their addiction typically attend therapy in addition to taking medication.

this helps reduce cravings and withdrawal symptoms by satisfying the desire to use. Naltrexone blocks these brain receptors so that addicts no longer feel a euphoric effect from any opioid drugs they subsequently take.

People trying to give up opioids typically engage in behavioral therapy in addition to taking medication. Therapy can help addicts change their attitudes and behaviors so that they can stay sober. It can also give them incentives to stay sober and helps build the life skills that they need to deal with stress, cravings, and triggers without relapsing into drug use. Therapy is important because while detoxing from opioids can happen in a matter of days, beating addiction takes much longer. Former addict Josh Moe explains, "I thought after 30 days in treatment, I would be 'cured' and back on the right path. But getting sober is not that easy." After multiple relapses, he says that he finally found himself on the path to recovery. He describes the process, saying, "I begrudgingly went back to inpatient care for another 30 days. From there I was sent to an extended care facility out of state for two months, then to a halfway house for another two months. I then went to a sober living house for nine months."[52] In total, Moe says that he was in supervised care for thirteen months.

"I thought after 30 days in treatment, I would be 'cured' and back on the right path. But getting sober is not that easy."[52]

—Josh Moe, former addict

RECOVERY IS NOT IMPOSSIBLE

While recovery from opioid addiction can be a long and difficult process, it is not impossible. The Wisconsin Department of Health Services explains that the path to recovery is different for every individual: "There are as many paths to health and wellness as there are people experiencing an opioid use disorder. Some people find success quitting opioids on their own with no supports from others. For most people, the path includes a combination of clinical supports and peer supports." For an addict stuck in addiction, that path might seem to be impossible. However, as the agency stresses, while the path to recovery might include ups and downs, it is never impossible. It insists, "Sustained recovery is within reach for everyone."[53]

CHAPTER FIVE

TRYING TO STOP A GROWING PUBLIC HEALTH CRISIS

In 2021, after steadily increasing for several years, the annual number of drug overdose deaths in the United States surpassed one hundred thousand. Nora Volkow, director of the National Institute on Drug Abuse, commented on this grim statistic, saying, "This is the highest number of drug overdoses in our country's history, and the numbers are climbing every month. There is an urgent need for a nationwide, coordinated response that a tragedy of this magnitude demands." According to Volkow, only a fraction of the people who struggle with opioid abuse receive treatment. She says, "Recent data from 2020 shows that only 13 percent of people with drug use disorders receive any treatment. Only 11 percent of people with opioid use disorder receive one of the three safe and effective medications that could help them quit and stay in recovery."[54]

Wider treatment is only one of the proposed solutions to the opioid epidemic. Other experts contend that the best way to address the problem is by reducing supply. Yet another suggestion is to remove the public stigma associated with opioid addiction. Overall, it is widely agreed that fentanyl and other synthetic opioids are part of a growing public health crisis and that the United States needs to take action to stop this crisis. However, there is disagreement over the best way to address this problem.

THE NEED FOR MORE TREATMENT

Like Volkow, many people believe that one of the most effective ways to reduce the opioid crisis is to get more people into treatment. However, in the United States, there are several barriers to doing so. One is that treatment can be expensive, and many people simply cannot afford it. Journalist German Lopez asked readers to share their addiction stories and ended up with more than one thousand responses. He says that one common theme among all these stories is that addiction treatment is expensive and extremely difficult to navigate. Many of the people who shared their experiences with him said that their insurance refused to provide treatment or only covered treatment at a low-quality facility, meaning that users suffering from addiction were unable to get effective help even if they wanted it. For instance, Lopez says, "Maureen O'Reilly lost her son to addiction after their health insurance plan wouldn't cover addiction care near home and he was sent to shoddy treatment facilities—some of which were later shut down—in Florida."[55] Some people reported spending tens of thousands of dollars to cover addiction treatment programs, something that is simply not an option for many others.

Another problem is that even for people able to cover the cost of treatment through insurance or by paying for it themselves, there is often nowhere to go for that treatment. Sarah Wakeman is the medical director for the Massachusetts General Hospital Substance Use Disorders Initiative and an

> "Maureen O'Reilly lost her son to addiction after their health insurance plan wouldn't cover addiction care near home and he was sent to shoddy treatment facilities."[55]
>
> —German Lopez, journalist

Addiction treatment can be expensive and insurance coverage extremely difficult to navigate, often leaving people stressed and frustrated.

assistant professor of medicine at Harvard Medical School. She says that the United States simply does not have enough addiction treatment facilities, stating, "In some parts of the country, patients have nowhere locally available to access effective treatment."[56] Even in places that do have treatment centers, there is typically not enough space for all the people who need help. Photojournalist Stephen Lam and reporter Trisha Thadani from the *San Francisco Chronicle* spent a year investigating fentanyl overdoses in that city. In an interview, Thadani shares the story of fentanyl addict Anthony Alexander, who wanted to quit but was not able to get the help he needed. She relates, "One day Anthony came to us and said, 'I'm going to go to the drop-in health center tomorrow.' And I said, 'Oh my God—we'll come with you. That's so exciting.' The next day, he got there and asked for detox. The nurse said, 'There are no beds today. There is nothing available.' And then he walked out." After being turned away, Alexander walked back out onto the street, found some fentanyl, and started smoking it right in front of the frustrated reporters. Thadani says, "It was just a glimpse into how deeply disjointed the system is. There was no one to even sit down and talk to Anthony about what the options were. We thought it was going to be the story of recovery and a guy overcoming these odds. Unfortunately, it ended up being another story about how things could have lined up for him if the system worked."[57]

REDUCING THE STIGMA THAT COMES WITH ADDICTION

Another barrier to treatment is that many addicts feel ashamed of their addiction and thus do not seek treatment. Dan Hill of Ohio responded to the *New York Times* request for reader stories relating to addiction. He points out that opioid addiction is frequently treated very differently than other medical problems, often causing addicts to feel embarrassed about what they are going through. He elaborates:

> Get cancer and you have a whole team of medical professionals working with you for years and through relapses. Plus, your medical bills are covered by insurance, your employer keeps you on the payroll and your medical insurance coverage continues. Friends and neighbors bring meals over for you, and prayer chains are instituted on your behalf. On the other hand, if you contract the disease of addiction, neither your family physician nor your local E.R. will treat you. Your employer fires you, and your medical coverage is discontinued. In most cases, even family members castigate you. You are viewed by most societal institutions as a sinner, a behavioral failure and someone unworthy of trust.[58]

This type of experience can make it very difficult for addicts to get treatment even if they work up the courage to try and do so.

An officer places handcuffs on a suspect during a drug raid. Some people argue that law enforcement could do a better job of reducing the supply of illegal opioids if it focused more attention on dealers of illicit drugs.

Critics insist that addiction is a disease and is not something to be ashamed of, and they argue that society needs to reduce the stigma associated with addiction so that people will be more willing to talk about the challenges they are facing and seek treatment. Those addicts, family members, and addiction experts interviewed by the *New York Times* echoed the claim that too many addicts do not seek help because of the stigma surrounding addiction. For example, Corinne Stinson from Atlanta, Georgia, says, "The shame and stigma behind addiction only force people deeper into the shadows."[59] She says that her sister was unable to get help because she could not escape that stigma.

MENTAL HEALTH TREATMENT

In addition to increasing treatment options and reducing the stigma associated with addiction, many experts argue that the United States can reduce opioid abuse by devoting more resources to mental health treatment. Research shows that many people who end up abusing opioids suffer from untreated mental illness. Therefore, if the United States wants to reduce opioid addiction, it needs to increase its treatment of mental illness, these experts say. The National Institutes of Health explains that mental illness raises the risk for opioid use disorder and says that a large percentage of people who struggle with the disorder also have mental illness.

The agency acknowledges that many do not receive treatment, often because there are simply not enough mental and behavioral health care providers. In a 2022 briefing the White House states, "Our country faces an unprecedented mental health crisis among people of all ages."[60] It explains that there is a considerable shortage of mental health providers and that more than a third of Americans live in areas that have fewer providers than the minimum needed for the size of their population.

Katherine Watkins is a psychiatrist and policy researcher at the RAND Corporation. She says that she previously worked at a residential treatment center and witnessed the lack of treatment availability. "You see how much many of them struggled and really tried, and we, as a healthcare system, weren't there," she says. "When they were ready, we were not there to help. We need to

THE WAR ON DRUGS IS NOT REDUCING DRUG USE

Since 1971 the US response to illegal drugs has been to wage war on them by increasing drug enforcement and imposing harsh penalties for drug offenders. However, despite more than fifty years of this so-called war on drugs, drug abuse remains a serious problem in the United States. Many users and dealers have gone to jail, but the drug trade has not suffered. As a result, many people argue that this policy is not effective. Kassandra Frederique, executive director of the Drug Policy Alliance, says, "The drug war is a failed policy and the things that they said would happen—people would stop using drugs, communities would get back together, we'd be safe, they'd get drugs off the street—those things didn't happen." Critics insist that the United States needs to try something else, such as focusing on treating addiction or addressing the conditions that cause people to sell and use drugs in the first place.

Quoted in Juhohn Lee, "America Has Spent over a Trillion Dollars Fighting the War on Drugs. 50 Years Later, Drug Use in the U.S. Is Climbing Again," CNBC, June 17, 2021. www.cnbc.com.

be there when they're ready." According to Watkins, treatment is extremely helpful for people who struggle with mental illness and opioid use disorder. She adds, "If they stay on treatment, they do better. They don't die. They don't have overdoses; they don't have suicide attempts. They get jobs."[61] Overall, she says, treatment helps a lot.

Most people agree that the COVID-19 pandemic made this problem worse for a few reasons. One is that social distancing caused isolation, boredom, and stress and thus increased mental health problems for many people. At the same time, it became even more difficult to get treatment for mental health problems. Both factors led to more people using opioids in an attempt to deal with their problems.

Reducing Supply

In addition to increasing treatment, experts argue that another effective way to address the opioid crisis is to reduce the supply of illegal synthetic opioids. However, policy makers have struggled to figure out exactly how to do so. According to the DEA, most

Holding Drug Companies Accountable

Some people argue that because opioid-producing drug companies played a role in creating the opioid epidemic, they should be held accountable. In recent years there have been several court cases in which judges and juries agreed, finding that drug companies and pharmacies contributed to the crisis by widely promoting opioids even though there was widespread evidence of the harm they caused. Some companies have been ordered to pay millions of dollars in damages to fund treatment and prevention services. For example, in 2022 Johnson & Johnson—which manufactured opioid drugs until 2020—and opioid drug wholesalers AmerisourceBergen, Cardinal Health, and McKesson agreed to pay $26 billion in total to settle lawsuits charging that they helped fuel the crisis. North Carolina state attorney general Josh Stein helped negotiate the deal. He says that this settlement will help with the problem and that "there will be people alive next year because of the programs and services we will be able to fund because of these settlement proceeds."

Quoted in Brian Mann, "4 U.S. Companies Will Pay $26 Billion to Settle Claims They Fueled the Opioid Crisis," NPR, February 25, 2022. www.npr.org.

of the fentanyl and fentanyl-related substances are smuggled or even mailed in from Mexico and China. Bryce Pardo, a policy researcher at the RAND Corporation, explains that drug traffickers continue to create potent new analogs that are extremely difficult to detect. He says:

> These are new chemicals in many cases that we just don't have the ability to detect. Some of the detection equipments at ports of entry just aren't trained on these new analogs because we've never seen [them] before. Same with canine units, canine units often may not be able to detect. We had to train the canine units to detect some of these newer synthetic opioids. . . . Before, the kind of analogy was trying to interdict heroin, at say, the port of entry or an international mail facility, it was like trying to find a needle in a haystack. Well, now with fentanyl, it's almost like trying to find a bacteria colony on that needle in that haystack, just much more complicated.[62]

As a result of the fact that new analogs are so difficult to detect, the United States has struggled to reduce the quantity of synthetic opioids that are smuggled into the country.

Other people argue that law enforcement should focus more attention on dealers of illicit drugs who knowingly distribute fentanyl or more potent analogs to unsuspecting customers. It is widely believed that most overdoses occur because people don't know there is fentanyl in the drugs they are buying or don't know how much fentanyl is in a product. Proponents of this theory argue that deaths could be reduced if law enforcement focused on trying to make dealers accountable for the dangers of the drugs they peddle. In a report for the Brookings Institution, Bryce Pardo and Peter Reuter argue, "Law enforcement should send an explicit message to dealers, informing them that they are responsible for keeping fentanyl out of the drug supply."[63] If dealers understand that punishment will certainly follow from selling fentanyl either intentionally or unintentionally, then it is believed that less fentanyl will reach users and fewer people will overdose. To make this happen, law enforcement must have more resources to quickly prosecute and close cases in which a clear trail of dangerous fentanyl leads back to a supplier.

Reducing Opioid Prescriptions

Another suggestion for reducing opioid use is to reduce opioid prescriptions. The United States has already tried to do this. In 2016 the CDC issued guidelines for the prescription of opioids, and in 2022 it updated those guidelines. The CDC recommends that doctors prescribe opioids only if alternative treatments are ineffective and only if the benefits are believed to outweigh the risks. The agency says, "Improving the way opioids are prescribed through clinical practice guidelines can ensure patients have access to safer, more effective pain treatment while reducing the number of people who potentially misuse or overdose from these drugs. Reducing exposure to prescription opioids, for situations where the risks of opioids outweigh the benefits, is a crucial part of prevention."[64] Research shows that these guidelines have led to a reduction in opioid prescriptions in the United States.

A doctor explains a prescription to her patient. While doctors have significantly reduced opioid prescriptions in recent years, opioid use has continued to increase in the United States.

However, there are many critics of this strategy who argue that it is causing substantial harm to people who rely on opioid prescriptions to manage chronic pain and other health conditions. Journalist Maia Szalavitz claims that cancer patients and people with chronic pain are suffering because doctors have dramatically reduced their opioid prescriptions in response to government pressure. Szalavitz and other critics argue that many people need opioids to manage pain and that reducing their prescriptions makes their lives extremely difficult. She says, "Research has shown that rather than reducing harm to patients, such cuts can dramatically increase their risk for suicide and overdose."[65]

Szalavitz and others point out that despite doctors significantly reducing opioid prescriptions in recent years, opioid use has increased, so this strategy does not seem to be helping. In 2021 the American Medical Association released a report stating that from 2011 to 2020 there was a 44 percent decrease in opioid prescriptions, yet drug overdose deaths have continued to rise. In fact, some experts argue that reducing prescriptions has fueled some of this rise because it has pushed people who formerly relied on those prescriptions to use illicit opioids instead.

A VITALLY IMPORTANT ISSUE

In its 2022 report, the Stanford-Lancet Commission stresses that opioids are ravaging the United States. The commission states, "Hundreds of thousands of individuals have fatally overdosed on prescription opioids, and millions more have become addicted to opioids or have been harmed in other ways, either as a result of their own opioid use or someone else's." Furthermore, the commission predicts that this problem will only get worse, arguing that "in the absence of any intervention, 1,220,000 fatal opioid overdoses will occur in the USA between 2020 and 2029."[66] The United States continues to struggle to find an effective way to deal with this crisis. However, doing so remains vitally important because the stakes are huge.

INTRODUCTION: WHEN EXPERIMENTATION BECOMES DEADLY

1. Quoted in Laura Santhanam, "Overdose Deaths Hit a Historic High in 2020. Frustrated Experts Say These Strategies Could Save Lives," *PBS NewsHour*, January 13, 2022. www.pbs.org.
2. Quoted in UCLA Health, "Adolescent Drug Overdose Deaths Rose Exponentially for the First Time in History During the COVID Pandemic," April 12, 2022. www.uclahealth.org.
3. Quoted in Erin McCormick, "Killed by a Pill Bought on Social Media: The Counterfeit Drugs Poisoning US Teens," *The Guardian* (Manchester, UK), December 23, 2001. www.theguardian.com.
4. Quoted in Summer Lin, "More Teenagers Dying from Fentanyl. 'It Has a Hold on Me, and I Don't Know Why,'" *Los Angeles Times*, November 12, 2022. www.latimes.com.
5. Quoted in US Drug Enforcement Administration, "DEA Recognizes National Fentanyl Prevention and Awareness Day," August 19, 2022. www.dea.gov.

CHAPTER ONE: ALL ABOUT SYNTHETIC OPIOIDS

6. American Cancer Society, "Opioids for Cancer Pain," January 3, 2019. www.cancer.org.
7. Quoted in Mike Benner, "Recovering Fentanyl Addict Speaks Out About Dangers of the Drug," KGW8, August 3, 2021. www.kgw.com.
8. Keith Humphreys et al., "Responding to the Opioid Crisis in North America and Beyond: Recommendations of the Stanford-Lancet Commission," *The Lancet*, February 2, 2022. www.thelancet.com.
9. Quoted in Jannelle Calderon, "Doctor Traces Fentanyl's Journey from Miracle Drug to Outsized Killer," Nevada Independent, August 26, 2022. https://thenevadaindependent.com.
10. Sarah Maslin Nir, "Inside Fentanyl's Mounting Death Toll: 'This Is Poison,'" *New York Times*, November 20, 2021. www.nytimes.com.

11. Quoted in Sarah S. Shin et al., "'It Wasn't Here, and Now It Is. It's Everywhere': Fentanyl's Rising Presence in Oregon's Drug Supply," *Harm Reduction Journal*, July 11, 2022. https://harmreductionjournal.biomed central.com.

12. Quoted in Raminta Daniulaityte et al., "'They Say It's Fentanyl, but They Honestly Look like Perc 30s': Initiation and Use of Counterfeit Fentanyl Pills," *Harm Reduction Journal*, May 25, 2022. https://harmreductionjournal .biomedcentral.com.

13. Ross Pomeroy, "A Coming Tidal Wave: The Opioid Epidemic Is About to Get a Whole Lot Worse," Big Think, August 2, 2022. https://bigthink.com.

14. John McMillan, ed., *American Epidemic: Reporting from the Front Lines of the Opioid Crisis.* New York: New Press, 2019, p. 7.

CHAPTER TWO: WHY ARE SYNTHETIC OPIOIDS DANGEROUS?

15. Quoted in Sally Hawkins et al., "Fentanyl Overdose Survivor Tells Her Story: 'I Was a Lucky One. I Gotta Make It Worth It,'" ABC News, April 6, 2022. https://abcnews.go.com.

16. Kathleen McLaughlin, "Underground Labs in China Are Devising Potent New Opiates Faster than Authorities Can Respond," *Science*, March 29, 2017. www.science.org.

17. US Drug Enforcement Administration, "Facts About Fentanyl." www.dea.gov.

18. Quoted in McMillan, *American Epidemic*, p. 230.

19. Jodie Martinson and Bridgette Watson, "Alive but Not the Same: B.C. Woman Survives Overdose but Left with Brain Damage," CBC News, November 2, 2019. www.cbc.ca.

20. Quoted in Martinson and Watson, "Alive but Not the Same."

21. Quoted in Greg Richter, "A 'Vicious Cycle' of Nonfatal Overdoses Causes 'Alzheimer's Like' Symptoms, Drexel Team Suggests," *Drexel News Blog*, December 8, 2021. https://newsblog.drexel.edu.

22. National Institute on Drug Abuse, "Prescription Opioids DrugFacts: What Are Prescription Opioids?," June 2021. https://nida.nih.gov.

23. American Psychiatric Association, "Opioid Use Disorder," 2022. https:// psychiatry.org.

24. American Psychiatric Association, "Opioid Use Disorder."

25. Quoted in *Frontline*, "Heroin & Opioid Addiction, in Your Own Words," PBS. www.pbs.org.

26. Eric Rankin, "The New Face of Fentanyl Addiction: Kati's Story," CBC, September 17, 2016. www.cbc.ca.

27. BoardPrep Recovery, "Fentanyl," July 14, 2020. www.boardpreprecovery .com.

28. Quoted in Daniulaityte et al., "'They Say It's Fentanyl, but They Honestly Look like Perc 30s.'"

29. BoardPrep Recovery, "Fentanyl."

30. Quoted in Richard Reeve, "A 20-Year-Old Minnesota Man Describes His Recovery from Addiction—as Experts Warn of Fentanyl's Deadly Effects," KSTP, August 26, 2022. https://kstp.com.

31. Quoted in Karen Feldscher, "What Led to the Opioid Crisis—and How to Fix It," Harvard T.H. Chan School of Public Health, February 9, 2022. www.hsph.harvard.edu.

CHAPTER THREE: HOW SYNTHETIC OPIOIDS ARE ALTERING SOCIETY

32. Quoted in Chris Adams, "The Fentanyl Surge," National Press Foundation, April 21, 2022. https://nationalpress.org.
33. United Nations Office on Drugs and Crime, *World Drug Report 2022*. Vienna: United Nations Office on Drugs and Crime, 2022. www.unodc.org.
34. HealthyChildren, "The Opioid Epidemic: How to Protect Your Family," January 12, 2023. www.healthychildren.org.
35. Quoted in Eden Davis, "Pushed into the Shadows: How Punishing Pregnant Women for Opioid Use Leads to More Birth Complications," ABC News, November 27, 2019. https://abcnews.go.com.
36. Quoted in *Frontline* "Heroin & Opioid Addiction, in Your Own Words."
37. Quoted in *Frontline* "Heroin & Opioid Addiction, in Your Own Words."
38. Marian Wright Edelman, "Children and the Opioid Crisis," Children's Defense Fund, October 27, 2017. www.childrensdefense.org.
39. Quoted in Alice Park, "Life After Addiction," *Time*, 2023. https://time.com.
40. Humphreys et al., "Responding to the Opioid Crisis in North America and Beyond."
41. Humphreys et al., "Responding to the Opioid Crisis in North America and Beyond."
42. Quoted in Anders Hagstrom, "Eric Adams Warns Fentanyl Will 'Destroy Generations' If New York Continues 'Sleeping on' Crisis," Fox News, January 26, 2023. www.foxnews.com.

CHAPTER FOUR: TREATING AND PREVENTING OVERDOSE AND ADDICTION

43. Quoted in Jonathon Gatehouse and Nancy Macdonald, "Fentanyl: The King of All Opiates, and a Killer Drug Crisis," *Maclean's*, June 22, 2015. www.macleans.ca.
44. Tyrone Riley, "What Is It like to Be Brought Back to Life?," Rescue Mission of Trenton, 2022. https://rescuemissionoftrenton.org.
45. Quoted in Change Grow Live, "Owen's Naloxone Story," 2023. www.changegrowlive.org.
46. Quoted in Liam Connolly, "Can Fentanyl Be Absorbed Through Your Skin?," UC Davis Health, October 18, 2022. https://health.ucdavis.edu.
47. Quoted in Steve Rummler Hope Network, "Callie's Naloxone Story," February 2, 2017. https://steverummlerhopenetwork.org.
48. National Institute on Drug Abuse, "Policy Brief: Naloxone for Opioid Overdose: Life-Saving Science," 2021. https://nida.nih.gov.
49. Bridget L. Hanson et al., "Preventing Opioid Overdose with Peer-Administered Naloxone: Findings from a Rural State," *Harm Reduction Journal*, January 9, 2020. https://harmreductionjournal.biomedcentral.com.

50. Giselle Appel et al., "Fentanyl Test Strips Empower People and Save Lives—So Why Aren't They More Widespread?," *Health Affairs*, June 2, 2021. www.healthaffairs.org.

51. Quoted in Mary Rose Madden, "In the Hole: The Problem with Fentanyl Test Strips . . . Fentanyl, Itself," WYPR, March 25, 2019. www.wypr.org.

52. Josh Moe, "A Full-Time Job in Hell: My Journey in and Out of Opioid Addiction," HealthPartners, 2023. www.healthpartners.com.

53. Wisconsin Department of Health Services, "Dose of Reality: Opioids Treatment and Recovery," November 24, 2022. www.dhs.wisconsin.gov.

Chapter Five: Trying to Stop a Growing Public Health Crisis

54. Nora Volkow, "Making Addiction Treatment More Realistic and Pragmatic: The Perfect Should Not Be the Enemy of the Good," National Institute on Drug Abuse, January 4, 2022. https://nida.nih.gov.

55. German Lopez, "1,000 People Sent Me Their Addiction Treatment Stories. Here's What I Learned," Vox, December 30, 2019. www.vox.com.

56. Quoted in Association of American Medical Colleges, "21 Million Americans Suffer from Addiction. Just 3,000 Physicians Are Specially Trained to Treat Them," December 18, 2019. www.aamc.org.

57. Quoted in Lisa Aliferis, "Patience, Commitment Help Journalists Capture Harsh Realities of Fentanyl Addiction," California Health Care Foundation, April 1, 2022. www.chcf.org.

58. Quoted in Jennifer Harlan, "'You Can Make It Out': Readers Share Stories of Opioid Addiction and Survival," *New York Times*, December 27, 2018. www.nytimes.com.

59. Quoted in Harlan, "'You Can Make It Out.'"

60. White House, "Fact Sheet: President Biden to Announce Strategy to Address Our National Mental Health Crisis, as Part of Unity Agenda in His First State of the Union," March 1, 2022. www.whitehouse.gov.

61. Quoted in National Institutes of Health HEAL Initiative, "When Addiction and Mental Illness Collide," November 10, 2022. https://heal.nih.gov.

62. Quoted in Adams, "The Fentanyl Surge."

63. Bryce Pardo and Peter Reuter, "Enforcement Strategies for Fentanyl and Other Synthetic Opioids," Brookings Institution, 2020. www.brookings.edu.

64. Centers for Disease Control and Prevention, "Improve Opioid Prescribing," October 30, 2019. www.cdc.gov.

65. Maia Szalavitz, "Doctors Prescribing Opioids in Good Faith Should Not Be Prosecuted," *Scientific American*, February 25, 2022. www.scientificamerican.com.

66. Humphreys et al., "Responding to the Opioid Crisis in North America and Beyond."

American Psychological Association

www.apa.org

The American Psychological Association represents American psychologists who study and treat human behavior. The association's website features information and resources about opioid abuse, including discussions of treatment options.

National Institute on Drug Abuse

https://nida.nih.gov

Founded in 1974, the National Institute on Drug Abuse is a federal organization that works to advance scientific research on drug use and addiction. Its website contains infographics, research reports, and fact sheets about synthetic opioid use in the United States.

Substance Abuse and Mental Health Services Administration (SAMHSA)

www.samhsa.gov

SAMHSA is an agency in the US Department of Health and Human Services that works to reduce the impact of substance abuse and mental illness in the United States. Its website contains information about opioid abuse and overdosing, as well as treatment options.

US Department of Health and Human Services

www.hhs.gov

The US Department of Health and Human Services was created to enhance the health and well-being of Americans by providing health services and promoting research. Its website contains information about opioid addiction and treatment, as well as statistics about the opioid epidemic in the United States.

US Drug Enforcement Administration (DEA)

www.dea.gov

Established in 1973, the DEA is the federal organization in charge of enforcing the controlled substances laws of the United States. Its website contains information about opioids and the illegal opioid market.

Books

John McMillian, ed., *American Epidemic: Reporting from the Front Lines of the Opioid Crisis*. New York: New Press, 2019.

Sam Quinones, *The Least of Us: True Tales of America and Hope in the Time of Fentanyl and Meth*. New York: Bloomsbury, 2021.

Brodie Ramin, *The Age of Fentanyl: Ending the Opioid Epidemic*. Toronto: Dundurn, 2020.

Ben Westhoff, *Fentanyl, Inc.: How Rogue Chemists Are Creating the Deadliest Wave of the Opioid Epidemic*. New York: Atlantic Monthly Press, 2019.

Internet Sources

Centers for Disease Control and Prevention, "Understanding the Opioid Overdose Epidemic," June 1, 2011. www.cdc.gov.

Keith Humphreys et al., "Responding to the Opioid Crisis in North America and Beyond: Recommendations of the Stanford-Lancet Commission," *The Lancet*, February 2, 2022. www.thelancet.com.

Sarah Maslin Nir, "Inside Fentanyl's Mounting Death Toll: 'This Is Poison,'" *New York Times*, November 20, 2021. www.nytimes.com.

Mayo Clinic, "How Opioid Addiction Occurs," April 12, 2022. www.mayoclinic.org

National Harm Reduction Coalition, "Fentanyl Use and Overdose Prevention Tips," September 8, 2020. https://harmreduction.org.

INDEX

percentage of illicit prescription drugs containing, 4
rainbow, 28
use of stimulants in combination with, 16
fentanyl test strips, 41–43
Food and Drug Administration, US, 43
Franklin, Ricardo, 11
Friedman, Joseph, 5, 6

Gupta, Rahul, 5

Hardee, Paris, 33–34
harm reduction, 43
HEAL Initiative (National Institutes of Health), 31
HealthyChildren (website), 29–30
heroin, 8, 11
fentanyl combined with, 15–16
lethal dose of, **20**
Hill, Dan, 49
Hoffman, Jan, 21
hydrocodone (Vicodin), 11

International Journal of Drug Policy, 22

Janssen, Paul, 15
Journal of the American Medical Association, 30

Kentucky, opioid abuse in, 31
King, Nikki, 31
Koh, Howard K., 26

life expectancy, decline in, 27
Long, Crystal, 12
Lopez, German, 47

Marshall, Kristen, 24
Martinson, Jodie, 21–22
Mather, Kati, 25
McLaughlin, Kathleen, 19
McMillan, John, 17
methadone, 43–44
methamphetamine, 17
Milgram, Anne, 7, 28
Moe, Josh, 44–45
Monitoring the Future survey (National Institute on Drug Abuse), 5

Morton, Michael, 36

naloxone (Narcan), 38–39, **41**
controversy over, 40–41
naltrexone, 43, 44
National Center for Injury Prevention and Control (Centers for Disease Control and Prevention), 27
National Harm Reduction Coalition, 43
National Institute on Drug Abuse, 5, 22, 60
on naloxone, 40
National Institutes of Health, 31, 51
neonatal abstinence syndrome (NAS), 29
neonatal opioid withdrawal syndrome (NOWS), 29–30
New York Times (newspaper), 50

opioid crisis
economic costs of, 30–31
high-risk groups for, 34–35
phases of, 13–17
as public health crisis, 26
opioids, 8
drug companies' promotion of, 12
effects of, 9
medical uses for, 11
natural, 9–10
number of deaths involving, 20
reducing prescriptions for, 54–55
semisynthetic, 11
See also synthetic opioids
opioid use disorder
definition of, 22–23
percentage of opioid users developing, 24
prevalence of, 7
O'Reilly, Maureen, 47
overdoses, 37–38
deaths from, 20
nonfatal, health effects of, 21–22
treating, **38**, 38–40
oxycodone (OxyContin/Percocet), 11

Pardo, Bryce, 53–54
Peder, Brooke, 21